Looking at Nature

Same or Different?

Bobbie Kalman

Dalmatian Press

Created by Bobbie Kalman

Published in 2013 by Dalmatian Press, LLC, Franklin, TN 37068-2068.
1-866-418-2572. DalmatianPress.com
Printed in the U.S.A.

CE16327/1012

Author and Editor-in-Chief
Bobbie Kalman

Editors
Reagan Miller
Robin Johnson

Photo research
Crystal Sikkens

Illustrations
Barbara Bedell: p. 14, 15, 24 (giraffe and porcupine)
Katherine Berti: p. 24 (snake)

Photographs
© Dreamstimer.com: p. 19 (bottom), 23 (bottom), 24 (fish)
© iStockphoto.com: p. 19 (top), 20 (middle)
© Shutterstock.com: p. 4–13 (except butterfly), 14-18, 20 (top), 21 (fly and cats eye), 22, 23 (top and middle), 24 (all except dog and fish)
Other images by Creatas, Digital Vision, and Photodisc

Contents

Look closely!

Many things in our world may look the same. Many things in our world may look different. Look closely at the things around you. Some things may be the same in some ways, but they may be very different in other ways. Look at the animals on this page. They are all cats. How are they the same? How are they different?

lynx cub

tiger cub

domestic kitten

The animals on this page are all insects. Insects are small animals with six legs. Some insects have wings. Look at all these insects. There are two of each kind of insect. Which insects are the same?

1

2

3

4

5

6

Answers: 1 and 4 are butterflies; 2 and 5 are dragonflies; 3 and 6 are praying mantises

Same or different?

This animal has white fur on its back. It also has some brown fur on its body. What can this animal be? Will it show itself to me?

Is this the same animal, or is it a different one? Look at both pictures. Give reasons why you think this lemur is the same animal as the one on page 6.

Are they birds?

A hummingbird is a small bird. It drinks nectar. Nectar is a sweet liquid in flowers. A hummingbird's long beak can reach the nectar in flowers. To stay in place while it drinks, a hummingbird flaps its wings quickly.

hummingbird

The animal above is also drinking nectar from a flower. It flaps its wings very fast, too. Is this animal a hummingbird? No, this animal is not a bird. It is an insect called a hummingbird moth. How do you think this insect got its name?

Be it a bee?

Bees are black insects with yellow stripes on their bodies. Bees have wings for flying. They visit flowers for nectar. Bees drink nectar and use it to make honey.

This bee is visiting a yellow flower.

bee

This animal has yellow stripes, too. It is looking at some yellow flowers. Is it the same as a bee, or is it different?
Can this animal fly? Can it make honey?
No, it cannot make honey.
This animal is a dog,
not a bee!

dog

Are these snakes?

This green snake is hiding among some leaves. It has a long body and smooth skin. Does it see another green snake on the next page? Do you see one?

caterpillar

Is this animal a green snake? Can a snake turn into a butterfly? No, it cannot, but a caterpillar can! This animal is a caterpillar, not a snake.

Long necks?

A giraffe has a very long neck and four long legs. It is a tall animal! A giraffe's brown fur has white markings on it. Giraffes live in hot, grassy places.

giraffe coat

giraffe

This animal's long body looks like a giraffe's neck. Its skin is also brown with white markings. Is this animal a giraffe? No, this animal is a moray eel. A moray eel is a fish that lives in the ocean. It has no neck. It has no legs. A moray eel has a long, thin body like the body of a snake.

moray eel

moray eel skin

A cup of what?

All these animals are small. They are so small that they can fit into teacups! How are these animals the same? How are they different?

This animal is a duck. A duck is a bird. Birds have two legs and two wings. Birds have feathers.

duck

dog

This little animal is a dog. A dog has four legs. It has fur on its body.

frog

This cup has a frog in it.
A frog has four legs.
A frog has smooth skin.
A frog does not have fur
or feathers on its body.

hamster

This furry little hamster
has four legs. Which other
animal has fur and four legs?
Which animal is most like
this hamster?

Ouch! That is sharp!

Porcupines are animals that have quills on their bodies. Quills are sharp needles. The quills keep porcupines safe from other animals. If an animal attacks a porcupine, the porcupine's quills get stuck in the animal's body. Ouch!

porcupine

porcupinefish

This animal has sharp needles on its body, too. When the animal is afraid, it fills its body with water, and its needles stick out. Is this animal the same as the porcupine on page 18? No, this animal is a porcupinefish.

Are eyes the same?

Look at the eyes on these pages. Are they the same or different? One pair is not really eyes. Which pair?

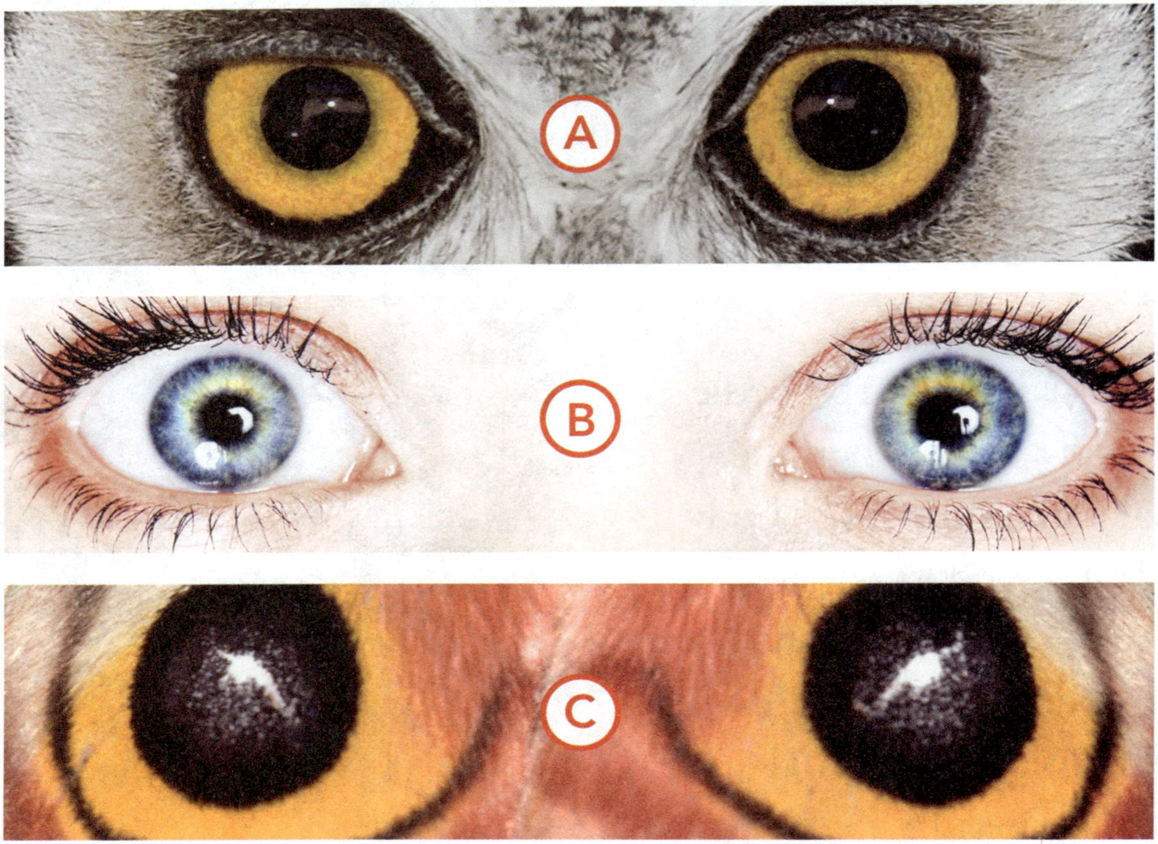

Each pair of eyes belongs to an animal. Match the eyes to the correct animal.

1. moth
2. fly
3. person
4. frog
5. owl
6. cat

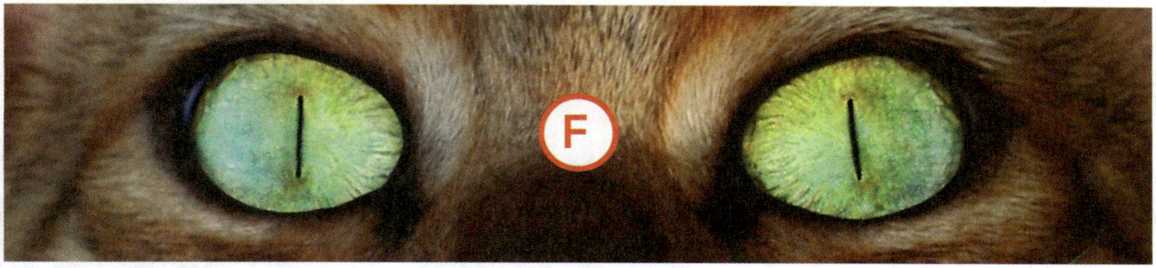

The spots on the moth's wings are not eyes. The spots are called eyespots. They look like eyes, but the moth does not use these eyes to see.

Answers: 1. moth–C; 2. fly–E; 3. person–B; 4. frog–D; 5. owl–A; 6. cat–F

A lot of leopards!

Leopards are wild cats. Leopards have many spots on their fur. This leopard cub is covered in spots. Some other animals have the word "leopard" in their names. Are they the same as this leopard cub, or are they different?

leopard

leopard gecko

This leopard gecko is covered with spots. Is it the same as the leopard cub? Does the gecko have fur? Is it a cat? No, this leopard gecko is a lizard. It is not the same as the leopard cub.

leopard butterfly

This butterfly is a leopard lacewing butterfly. Is it the same as the leopard cub? Can the leopard cub fly?

leopard shark

This leopard shark is a fish. It lives in the ocean. Is it the same as the leopard cub? How is it different?

Index

Other index words